P9-ELS-758

19.95

U.S. Coast Guard

BY LINDA BOZZO

Cuyahoga Falls
Library
Cuyahoga Falls, Ohio

amicus
high interest

Amicus High Interest is an imprint of Amicus
P.O. Box 1329, Mankato, MN 56002
www.amicuspublishing.us

Copyright © 2014 Amicus. International copyright reserved in
all countries. No part of this book may be reproduced in any
form without written permission from the publisher.

Library of Congress Cataloging-in-Publication Data
Bozzo, Linda.
 U.S. Coast Guard / by Linda Bozzo.
    pages cm. -- (Serving in the military)
 Includes index.
 Summary: "An introduction to what the US Coast Guard
is, what recruits do, and jobs soldiers could learn. Includes
descriptions of missions to rescue a sailor in a storm and
directing boat traffic after the 9/11 attacks on New York
City"--Provided by publisher.
 Audience: Grades K-3.
 ISBN 978-1-60753-393-1 (library binding) -- ISBN 978-1-
60753-441-9 (ebook)
 1. United States. Coast Guard--Juvenile literature. I. Title.
 VG53.B67 2014
 363.28'60973--dc23
                            2013001426

Editor   Wendy Dieker
Series Designer   Kathleen Petelinsek
Page production   Red Line Editorial, Inc.

Photo Credits
US Coast Guard Photo/Alamy, cover; Seaman Amanda
Miles/U.S. Coast Guard, 5; Petty Officer 2nd Class Walter
Shinn/U.S. Coast Guard, 6; Lt. Zach Huff/U.S. Coast Guard,
9; U.S. Coast Guard, 10; CWO Donnie Brzuska/U.S. Coast
Guard, 13; Petty Officer 1st Class Lauren Jorgensen/U.S.
Coast Guard, 15; Petty Officer 1st Class Luke Pinneo/U.S.
Coast Guard, 16; Petty Officer 3rd Class William B. Mitchell/
U.S. Coast Guard, 19; Petty Officer 1st Class Tasha Tully/U.S.
Coast Guard, 20; Petty Officer Patrick Kelley/U.S. Coast
Guard, 22; Petty Officer Seth Johnson/U.S. Coast Guard, 24;
Petty Officer 3rd Class Stephen Lehmann/U.S. Coast Guard,
27; Petty Officer 3rd Class Barbara L. Patton/U.S. Coast
Guard, 28

Printed in the United States at Corporate Graphics in North
Mankato, Minnesota
5-2013 / 1150

Table of Contents

Call the Coast Guard   4

Learning the Ropes   **11**

The Home Front   18

Working Overseas   25

Serving Our Country   **29**

Glossary   30

Read More   **31**

Websites   **31**

Index   32

6669

Call the Coast Guard

It is October 29, 2012. *H.M.S. Bounty* is out at sea. It is sailing near North Carolina. Hurricane Sandy is coming up the east coast. Strong winds toss the ship. The ship's power goes out. The *Bounty* is sinking! The crew is in danger! They send a **distress signal**. The U.S. Coast Guard gets the call. Help is on the way!

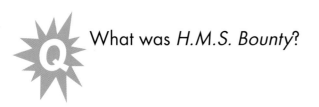 What was *H.M.S. Bounty*?

A U.S. Coast Guard helicopter flies out to help a sinking boat.

 It was a ship with three masts. It was built to look like a ship from the 1700s.

The coast guard plane finds the ship. The crew is in a life raft. But the captain and another sailor were swept away. The coast guard sends a rescue chopper. A rescue swimmer drops into the giant waves. He helps the sailors one by one. They are lifted to safety.

A rescue swimmer drops into water to save stranded people.

The chopper heads back to the Coast Guard Air Station. The *Bounty* crew is safe on land. But the coast guard's job is not over yet. The coast guard must look for the two missing people. They find the sailor, but she did not survive. The captain has not been found. No one knows where he is.

Coast guardsmen help an *H.M.S. Bounty* sailor back on land.

8

Coast guardsmen unload drugs they took from criminals.

 Q Does the Coast Guard only work near the ocean?

Learning the Ropes

The U. S. Coast Guard is one of the U.S. Armed Forces. The coast guard works along coastlines and waterways. They are famous for rescue missions. But they do a lot to protect U.S. waters. They help keep drugs and crime out of our country. There is a lot to learn to work in the coast guard.

 No. They also take care of major rivers and the Great Lakes.

New members of the coast guard are called **recruits**. They must love to swim. They train to swim long and hard. They learn to use pistols and rifles. Some recruits train to dive under the water. Others learn to fly planes. Recruits who finish basic training are called coast guardsmen. Even women get that name.

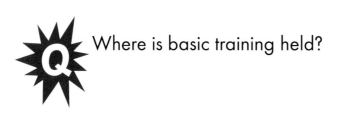 Where is basic training held?

Recruits must work hard to be fit.

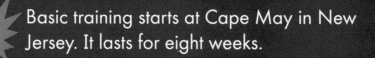

A Basic training starts at Cape May in New Jersey. It lasts for eight weeks.

After basic training, the work starts. Some coast guardsmen drive boats and ships. Some fight fires on the sea. Some load and unload goods from ships. Others make sure boaters follow U.S. laws. Still others train to become officers. They lead other coast guardsmen.

Officers work together to make plans for their crew.

Have you ever wanted to work on a boat? You could do search and rescue. How about working to keep U.S. waters clean? You could catch people dumping pollution in the water. If you want to fly, you could fly a rescue plane. Want to stay on the ground? There are jobs on the shore to do. You could control air traffic.

These guardsmen work at a command center on shore.

The Home Front

The coast guard is always ready to help. Search and rescue is a big part of their job. They save about 10 people a day. They are always busy. The coast guard also helps when disaster strikes. Floods and hurricanes happen along the coasts. People can be trapped! The coast guard rescues people from danger.

The coast guard looks for people who need help in a flooded river.

A guardsman helps pull a bouy out of the water.

Q Why are **buoys**, lighthouses, **beacons**, and **fog signals** important?

The coast guard works to keep water safe. They keep buoys lit. They check lighthouses. They fix broken beacons. Fog signals must always work.

The coast guard enforces laws. There are fishing laws. There are laws against illegal drugs. Many types of water pollution are illegal. The coast guard arrests people who break our laws.

 They help boats find their way in the dark or fog. Captains can see the lights on buoys and the shore. They can hear the fog signals.

The coast guard sends ships to break ice in frozen waterways.

The U.S. Coast Guard keeps our water clean. They help clean up after an oil spill. Animals and plants need clean water to live in.

The coast guard also keeps water safe for travel. Sometimes waterways freeze over. Ships can't get through. The coast guard has ships called **icebreakers** that break the ice. They once made a path for a ship that carried fuel to Alaska.

A coast guard boat watches for enemies around a U.S. Navy ship.

Q Does the U.S. Coast Guard ever fight?

Working Overseas

Sometimes the president sends the coast guard overseas. This can happen during war. It could also be for special missions. The coast guard works for the U.S. Navy at these times. They help watch for enemies. They search enemy ships for weapons.

Sometimes. But it is not their main job. Protecting **ports** and **harbors** is what they do the most.

The coast guard also helps move U.S. troops and supplies overseas. Special units guard ports in other countries. They protect other U.S. ships. Guardsmen also help train foreign troops. They help keep the peace. They might help clean up after a disaster. The coast guard is always ready to help.

A crew moves supplies to
help Haiti after a disaster.

Serving Our Country

In 2001, enemies attacked New York City. They flew planes into buildings. People panicked! The U.S. Coast Guard was ready to help! They helped people get out of the city. They helped boats get through the smoky harbor. We can always count on the U.S. Coast Guard!

The coast guard patrols New York Harbor.

Glossary

beacon A beam of light that guides ships at night.

buoy A floating object in a body of water that helps guide boats.

distress signal A radio call to let people know a boat is in danger.

fog signal A sound signal that is used to guide ships when there is fog.

harbor A place on the shore where ships load and unload cargo.

icebreaker A ship that breaks up ice so other ships can travel.

port A place near shore where ships can dock or anchor safely.

recruit A person who has just joined the military.

Read More

Goldish, Meish. *Coast Guard: Civilian to Guardian.* New York, NY. Bearport Publishing, 2011.

Markovics, Joyce L.. *Today's Coast Guard Heroes.* New York, NY. Bearport Publishing, 2012.

Randolph, Joanne. *Coast Guard Boats.* New York, NY. PowerKids Press, 2008.

Websites

A Day with the Coast Guard coloring book
http://www.uscg.mil/top/downloads/coloring.asp

Brain Pop: Armed Forces
http://www.brainpop.com/socialstudies/ usgovernmentandlaw/armedforces/preview.weml

United States Coast Guard
http://www.gocoastguard.com/

Index

beacons 20, 21

buoys 20, 21

Cape May Training Center 13

disasters 18, 26

drugs 11, 21

fog signals 20, 21

helicopters 7, 8

H.M.S. Bounty 4, 5, 7, 8

Hurricane Sandy 4

icebreakers 23

jobs 8, 14, 17, 18, 25

lighthouses 20, 21

missions 11, 18, 25, 26, 29

officers 14

oil spills 23

pollution 17, 21

recruits 12

rescue swimmer 7

training 12, 13, 14, 26

war 25

weapons 12, 25

About the Author

Linda Bozzo is the author of more than 30 books for the school and library market. Visit her website at www.lindabozzo.com. She would like to thank all of the men and women in the military for their outstanding service to our country. She would like to dedicate this book to all of the victims of Hurricane Sandy.